TEAM SPIRIT®

SMART BOOKS FOR YOUNG FANS

THE WASHINGTON NATIONALS

BY

MARK STEWART

NORWOOD HOUSE PRESS

CHICAGO, ILLINOIS

Norwood House Press
P.O. Box 316598
Chicago, Illinois 60631

For information regarding Norwood House Press, please visit our website at:
www.norwoodhousepress.com or call 866-565-2900.

All photos courtesy of Getty Images except the following:
SportsChrome (4, 12, 14, 27, 32), Topps, Inc. (6, 7, 10, 17, 20, 34 top, 36, 37, 38, 41 & 42 top),
Black Book Partners Archives (11, 18, 21 top, 22, 27, 28, 39, 40, 42 bottom left, 43 left & 45),
Montreal Expos (15), Author's Collection (33 & 43 bottom right),
O-Pee-Chee Ltd. (43 top right), Matt Richman (48).
Cover Photo: John McDonnell via Getty Images

The memorabilia and artifacts pictured in this book are presented for educational and informational purposes,
and come from the collection of the author.

Editor: Mike Kennedy
Designer: Ron Jaffe
Project Management: Black Book Partners, LLC.
Special thanks to Topps, Inc.

Library of Congress Cataloging-in-Publication Data

Stewart, Mark, 1960-
  The Washington Nationals / by Mark Stewart. -- Library ed.
     p. cm. -- (Team spirit)
  Includes bibliographical references and index.
  Summary: "A Team Spirit Baseball edition featuring the Washington
Nationals that chronicles the history and accomplishments of the team.
Includes access to the Team Spirit website, which provides additional
information, updates and photos"--Provided by publisher.
  ISBN 978-1-59953-501-2 (library : alk. paper) -- ISBN 978-1-60357-381-8
(ebook) 1. Washington Nationals (Baseball team)--History--Juvenile
literature. I. Title.
  GV875.W27S84 2012
  796.357'6409753--dc23
                                        2011047978

Manufactured in the United States of America in North Mankato, Minnesota.
196N—012012

COVER PHOTO: It's high-fives all around after a win by the Nationals in 2011.

TABLE OF CONTENTS

ABOUT OUR GLOSSARY

In this book, there may be several words that you are reading for the first time. Some are sports words, some are new vocabulary words, and some are familiar words that are used in an unusual way. All of these words are defined on page 46. Throughout the book, sports words appear in **bold type**. Regular vocabulary words appear in ***bold italic type***.

MEET THE
NATIONALS

Building a winning team in baseball is one of the greatest challenges in all of sports. Doing this in a new city is even harder. The Washington Nationals are showing the world how it's done. It takes time and patience, plus talent. It also takes a little luck.

The Nationals mix exciting new hitters and pitchers with faces that are familiar to their fans. The older stars teach the younger ones. The younger ones remind the experienced players that baseball can be fun. Luck hasn't always been on Washington's side, but the "Nats" always seek the best talent for their lineup.

This book tells the story of the Nationals. They started with another name, in another city, in another country. Back then, many of their fans also spoke another language! But good baseball sounds the same wherever it is played.

Young pitcher Drew Storen gives Ivan Rodriguez a high five. Rodriguez is one of many experienced stars who have worn the Washington uniform.

5

GLORY DAYS

Washington, D.C. is the capital of the United States. That is why it seemed so strange that the city went without a baseball home team for almost 35 years. After the 1971 season, the Washington Senators left town and became the Texas Rangers. Not until 2005 did baseball return to Washington. The team that brought

it back was the Montreal Expos.

The Expos played their first season in 1969. That year, the **National League (NL)** added two teams, one in San Diego, California and the other in the Canadian city of Montreal. Two years earlier, Montreal had held a successful World's Fair called Expo 67. The city would also host the *Summer Olympics* in 1976. Montreal was truly an *international* city, and **Major League Baseball (MLB)** was excited about the idea of bringing the game to a wider audience.

The Expos put good players on the field right away. Their stars included Bill Stoneman, Rusty Staub, Ron Fairly, Mack Jones, and Steve Renko. Just a few games into the 1969 season, Stoneman pitched a **no-hitter** against the Philadelphia Phillies. Over the next few years, many more talented players wore the Montreal uniform, including Mike Torrez, Mike Marshall, Ken Singleton, and Ron Hunt.

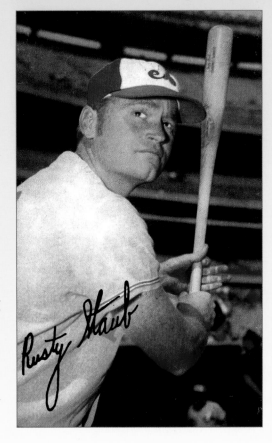

By the late 1970s, the Expos had assembled a very competitive team. Catcher Gary Carter, third baseman Larry Parrish, and outfielders Warren Cromartie, Ellis Valentine, and Andre Dawson formed the heart of a very dangerous batting order. At the same time, Montreal developed an excellent pitching staff, which was led by Steve Rogers, Scott Sanderson, Bill Gullickson, Charlie Lea, and Jeff Reardon.

Over the years, the Expos welcomed many other star players, including Tim Raines, Tim Wallach, Andres Galarraga, and Dennis Martinez. Despite all of this talent, the team had a hard time winning on a regular basis. Montreal made the playoffs just once, in 1981.

LEFT: This trading card shows the 1969 Expos.   **ABOVE**: Rusty Staub led Montreal in home runs in each of the team's first three seasons.

The team won a playoff series against the Phillies but then lost the **National League Championship Series (NLCS)** to the Los Angeles Dodgers.

The Expos rose again in the 1990s. Those teams were paced by hitters Larry Walker, Moises Alou, and Marquis Grissom. Pitchers Pedro Martinez, Ken Hill, and John Wetteland were stars on the mound. In 1994, Montreal had the best team in baseball. The Expos seemed headed to the **World Series** until the season ended in August over a *labor dispute*.

Heartbroken and frustrated, many Montreal fans stopped following the Expos. That was a shame, because they missed a chance to watch Vladimir Guerrero. The slugging outfielder was named an **All-Star** in 1999 and later developed into the league's best all-around star. Unfortunately, the team could not afford to pay its players the huge salaries that other clubs offered. Guerrero and other top *prospects* eventually left Montreal for other teams.

In 2002, with the Expos struggling to stay in business, MLB took over the team. Three years later, the club moved to Washington, D.C. and

LEFT: Pedro Martinez
ABOVE: Vladimir Guerrero

was renamed the Nationals. In their first season, the Nats put a good team on the field. They had stars from the Expos, including Nick Johnson, Jose Vidro, Brad Wilkerson, Chad Cordero, and Livan Hernandez. The Nationals also brought in new players, including Cristian Guzman, Jose Guillen, and Esteban Loiaza.

RYAN ZIMMERMAN
Third Base

Washington
Nationals®

In the years that followed, the Nationals added more well-known players, including Alfonso Soriano, Austin Kearns, Dmitri Young, Adam Dunn, and Jayson Werth. They gave Washington fans plenty of thrills. But it was the team's up-and-coming players who had everyone in the city buzzing about baseball.

Soon fans were showing up to the ballpark to cheer for young stars such as Ryan Zimmerman, Jordan Zimmermann, Wilson Ramos, Ian Desmond, Danny Espinosa, Drew Storen, Bryce Harper, Gio Gonzalez, and Stephen Strasburg. These players were eager to make the Nationals a winner. Before long, Washington became the talk of baseball.

ABOVE: Ryan Zimmerman
RIGHT: Stephen Strasburg fires a pitch. There was a buzz in the stands whenever he took the mound for the Nationals.

HOME TURF

When the team played its first game as the Expos, its home was Jarry Park Stadium in Montreal. Many fans remember home runs splashing into a city swimming pool beyond the right field fence. In 1977, the Expos moved into Olympic Stadium, which had been built for the 1976 Summer Olympics.

When the team became the Nationals, it originally played at Robert F. Kennedy Memorial Stadium. That had been the ballpark of the Washington Senators before they moved away in 1972. In 2008, Nationals Park opened. The stadium was built to reflect the Washington, D.C. area. It has beautiful views of many landmarks, including the Navy Yard. The Nats' ballpark is also one of the most environmentally friendly sports structures in the world.

BY THE NUMBERS

- The Nats' ballpark has 41,546 seats.
- The distance from home plate to the left field foul pole is 336 feet.
- The distance from home plate to the center field wall is 402 feet.
- The distance from home plate to the right field foul pole is 335 feet.

The view from the visiting team's dugout shows the big scoreboard in right field of the Nationals' stadium.

DRESSED FOR SUCCESS

W hen the Expos first took the field in 1969, they had a very "mod-looking" *logo*. The red, white, and blue *M* on their caps was actually a combination of three letters—*EMB*. Those letters stood for *Expos de Montréal Baseball*, the team's name in French. The Expos used that *M* and the team colors for all 36 seasons they played in Canada.

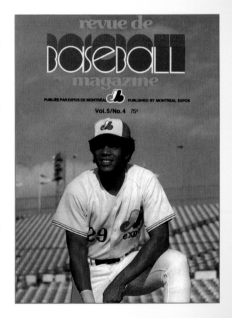

The Nationals kept those colors. They also added touches of gold. The Nationals like to use many different color combinations in their uniforms. Some are very modern. Others are historic. For most games, however, red has been the main uniform color.

The team's logo includes nine stars. They stand for the nine positions on a baseball field. The logo also spells out the team's name in capital letters.

LEFT: Jordan Zimmermann wears one of the team's 2011 home uniforms.
ABOVE: Ken Singleton models Montreal's uniform on the cover of a 1970s French-language game program.

The Expos began building a strong core of talent in their early years. By the end of the 1970s, they had one of the best teams in baseball. The Expos came very close to winning the **NL East** in 1979 and 1980. Both times they were beaten out in the final weekend of the season, first by the Pittsburgh Pirates and then by the Philadelphia Phillies. In 1981, the Expos were 30–25 and in third place when

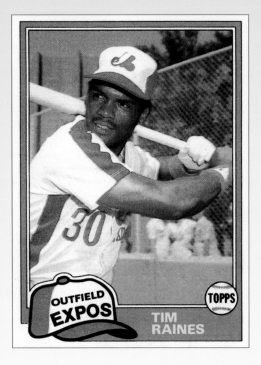

LEFT: You're out! Gary Carter makes a play at home plate in 1981.
RIGHT: Tim Raines stole 71 bases for Montreal as a rookie.

a baseball **_strike_** interrupted the season. The strike lasted more than seven weeks.

Montreal fans could hardly wait for the season to restart. Their team was led by young sluggers Gary Carter and Andre Dawson. The Expos also had a speedy **rookie** named Tim Raines. He batted over .300 and could steal a base any time he wanted.

Montreal's pitching was excellent, too. Steve Rogers and Bill Gullickson were two of the best starters in the league. A year earlier, Gullickson struck out 18 batters in a game. The team's **bullpen** was solid as well. During the season, the Expos traded for Jeff Reardon. When Reardon pitched at the end of close games, he made Montreal almost impossible to beat.

When the season resumed, it was announced that every team's record would start at 0–0. At the end of the year, the first-place team from the first half of the season would play the first-place team

from the second half. The Expos played well and finished one game ahead of the St. Louis Cardinals. They faced the Phillies for the NL East championship. The first team to win three games would move on to the NLCS and play for the **pennant**.

The Expos took the first two games, each by a score of 3–1. Rogers and Gullickson were brilliant, and Reardon **saved** both games. The Phillies did not give up easily. They had won the 1980 World Series and wanted a chance to repeat as champions. Philadelphia won the next game 6–2 and then tied the series with a 6–5 victory in extra innings in Game 4.

Rogers faced Philadelphia's top pitcher, Steve Carlton, in the final game. The Expos loaded the bases in the fifth inning, and Rogers came to bat. He shocked Carlton and the Phillies by hitting a single. Larry Parrish and Chris Speier scored to make the score 2–0. Parrish drove in another run one inning later.

Rogers pitched all nine innings and allowed just six hits and no runs. The last out of the game came on a line drive that was caught by first baseman Warren Cromartie. The Expos were NL East champions!

Sadly for Montreal fans, the team fell short of winning the pennant. They faced the Los Angeles Dodgers in the NLCS and lost three games to two. Game 5 was a tense battle that Los Angeles won 2–1 on a run in the ninth inning. When the Expos left Montreal and became the Nationals 24 years later, the team still had not played in a World Series.

LEFT: Andre Dawson led the team in hits and home runs in 1981.
ABOVE: Steve Rogers delivers a pitch to home plate.

GO-TO GUYS

To be a true star in baseball, you need more than a quick bat and a strong arm. You have to be a "go-to guy"—someone the manager wants on the pitcher's mound or in the batter's box when it matters most. Fans of the Expos and the Nationals have had a lot to cheer about over the years, including these great stars …

THE PIONEERS

STEVE ROGERS   Pitcher

• BORN: 10/26/1949   • PLAYED FOR TEAM: 1973 TO 1985

When the Expos needed a victory, they handed the ball to Steve Rogers. He led the NL in **shutouts** twice and almost never missed a start. Rogers had an unusual style. He seemed to stumble after delivering every pitch.

GARY CARTER   Catcher

• BORN: 4/8/1954   • PLAYED FOR TEAM: 1974 TO 1984 & 1992

Gary Carter was an excellent defensive catcher and a great team leader. He played in the **All-Star Game** almost every year and hit well under pressure. Carter was the first Expo elected to the **Hall of Fame**.

ANDRE DAWSON   Outfielder

- BORN: 7/10/1954
- PLAYED FOR TEAM: 1976 TO 1986

Andre Dawson was nicknamed the "Hawk" for the way he hunted down deep drives in the outfield. He could also hit the ball a long way. Dawson was the only player to slam 200 home runs and steal 200 bases in an Expos uniform.

TIM RAINES   Outfielder

- BORN: 9/16/1959
- PLAYED FOR TEAM: 1979 TO 1990 & 2001

Tim Raines was the most exciting player on the Expos during the 1980s. He stole at least 70 bases six years in a row and was the NL batting champion in 1986.

TIM WALLACH   Third Baseman

- BORN: 9/14/1957
- PLAYED FOR TEAM: 1980 TO 1992

Tim Wallach came to the team after winning the Golden Spikes Award as America's best college baseball player. He was an All-Star five times for the Expos and won three **Gold Glove** awards for his excellent fielding. Wallach also led the NL in doubles twice.

LEFT: Gary Carter
TOP RIGHT: Andre Dawson
BOTTOM RIGHT: Tim Wallach

DENNIS MARTINEZ — Pitcher

- BORN: 5/14/1955
- PLAYED FOR TEAM: 1986 TO 1993

Dennis Martinez was the first big leaguer from the country of Nicaragua. He had many different pitches, and batters rarely got good swings against him. In 1991, Martinez threw a perfect game—27 batters, 27 outs—against the Los Angeles Dodgers.

PEDRO MARTINEZ — Pitcher

- BORN: 10/25/1971
- PLAYED WITH TEAM: 1994 TO 1997

Before Pedro Martinez was a star with the Boston Red Sox and New York Mets, he was the top pitcher on the Expos. He joined the team as a hard-throwing relief pitcher but soon became the NL's top starter. Martinez won the **Cy Young Award** in 1997.

VLADIMIR GUERRERO — Outfielder

- BORN: 2/9/1975   • PLAYED FOR TEAM: 1996 TO 2003

Vladimir Guerrero was one of the most talented and confident players the team ever had. No Montreal fan ever left the ballpark if Guerrero was due to bat one more time. Guerrero believed he could hit any pitch over the fence or throw out any baserunner—and he often did!

RYAN ZIMMERMAN   Third Baseman

- BORN: 9/28/1984
- FIRST YEAR WITH TEAM: 2005

Few young players have ever fielded and hit better than Ryan Zimmerman. He was known for his amazing plays at third base and his game-winning home runs. In 2009, Zimmerman set a team record with a 30-game hitting streak.

STEPHEN STRASBURG   Pitcher

- BORN: 7/20/1988
- FIRST YEAR WITH TEAM: 2010

Stephen Strasburg was the first player chosen in the 2009 baseball **draft**. One year later, he took the mound for the Nats and was blowing away batters in the big leagues. In 2011, Strasburg bounced back from an arm injury and picked up where he left off.

JAYSON WERTH   Outfielder

- BORN: 5/20/1979   • FIRST YEAR WITH TEAM: 2011

When Jayson Werth played for the Philadelphia Phillies, he showed that he could do it all. That is why the Nationals made him their highest-paid player before the 2011 season. In his first season in Washington, Werth became the team's best all-around player.

LEFT: Dennis Martinez
ABOVE: Ryan Zimmerman

CALLING THE SHOTS

For a team that has been around since only 1969, the Nationals have had some wonderful managers. During their years in Montreal, the Expos were led by Gene Mauch, Dick Williams, Buck Rodgers, and Felipe Alou. Each was among the most respected managers in baseball.

The team's last manager in Montreal was Frank Robinson. He was also the Nationals' first manager in Washington, D.C. During the 1950s and 1960s, he was one of the top all-around players in baseball. Robinson won the **Most Valuable Player (MVP)** award in the National League in 1961. Five years later, he was named the **American League** MVP. Both years he helped his team win the pennant.

Robinson knew when to take chances and when to play it safe. He was a smart player and a good teammate. In the 1970s, as his playing career came to an end, many thought he would be an excellent manager. In 1975, the Cleveland Indians hired Robinson as their **player-manager**. It marked the first time an African-American managed a big-league team. Robinson guided the San Francisco Giants and Baltimore Orioles before taking over the Expos in 2002.

Frank Robinson smiles for the camera during his days as the manager of the Nationals.

New teams often hire new managers for a fresh start. When the Expos moved to Washington in 2005, the team decided to keep a good thing going. Robinson had been managing Montreal for three seasons. In two of those years, the Expos had a winning record.

Robinson did an amazing job with the Nationals. They finished 81–81 in their first year even though the team did not have a roster full of stars. No one on the club batted .300, slugged more than 25 homers, or drove in more than 100 runs. But Robinson taught his players that avoiding mistakes was the key to winning. He stayed one more year before moving on. Robinson was followed in the dugout by other good managers, including Manny Acta, Jim Riggleman, and Davey Johnson.

ONE GREAT DAY

On June 9, 2009, the Nationals selected Stephen Strasburg with the first pick in the baseball draft. Exactly 364 days later—on June 8, 2010—Strasburg took the mound for Washington for the very first time. As a college pitcher, he had been almost unhittable. During his brief stay in the **minor leagues**, batters had no luck against him either. Strasburg had a fastball that reached 100 mph. His curve broke so sharply that hitters often missed it by a foot. Both pitches looked identical when they left his hand.

Despite his success in college and the minors, some experts predicted that Strasburg would struggle in the big leagues. They said that hitters in the majors would recognize his curve and not chase it as it dove out of the strike zone. The experts also said that enemy batters would be able to catch up to Strasburg's fastball.

Facing the Pittsburgh Pirates in front of a sellout crowd in Nationals Park, Strasburg proved those experts wrong. After retiring the first two Pittsburgh batters, he struck out the third to end the inning. In the

Stephen Strasburg prepares to throw his blazing fastball.

second inning, Strasburg struck out three batters. He struck out two more in the third inning.

In the fourth, Strasburg finally made a mistake. He tried to fool Delwyn Young with a **change-up**, but the Pittsburgh hitter drilled the pitch into the seats for a two-run homer. The fans watched to see how their young star would react. Strasburg pitched three more innings and did not allow another Pirate to reach first base.

Adam Dunn and Josh Willingham hit back-to-back home runs in the top of the seventh inning to give Strasburg a 4–2 lead. He struck out all three batters in the bottom of the inning. That gave him a total of 14 strikeouts for the day, just one short of the record for a pitcher in his first game. After the final out, Strasburg's teammates paid him the ultimate compliment—three shaving-cream pies to the face!

"I've been catching a lot of guys," said Ivan Rodriguez, who was behind the plate for the Nationals, "but this kid is unbelievable."

LEGEND HAS IT

WHICH WASHINGTON PLAYERS TOOK THE FIELD WITH SPELLING ERRORS ON THEIR UNIFORMS?

LEGEND HAS IT that Ryan Zimmerman and Adam Dunn did. There's an old saying that goes, "There's no *I* in *TEAM*." This may be true, but there is definitely an *O* in *NATIONALS*. In a 2009 game, Zimmerman and Dunn did not notice that the lettering on their new jerseys spelled out *NATINALS*. It wasn't their fault—the uniform-maker had made the mistake. After the error was discovered, both players went back into the locker room. While the Nats batted in the third inning, Zimmerman and Dunn changed into jerseys with correct spelling.

ABOVE: Adam Dunn warms up during a spring practice. He was one of two Washington players who were given uniforms with a spelling mistake.

WHO WAS THE FIRST U.S. PRESIDENT TO 'CALL' A HOME RUN?

LEGEND HAS IT that President George W. Bush was. On March 30, 2008, President Bush threw out the first pitch of the season at brand-new Nationals Park. Later he joined the broadcasters calling the game in their booth at the stadium. They asked President Bush to describe the action for television viewers. Moments later, Chipper Jones of the Atlanta Braves slugged a homer. President Bush knew a thing or two about baseball. Before getting into politics, he was the owner of the Texas Rangers.

WHO HAD THE BEST TEAM IN BASEBALL IN 1994?

LEGEND HAS IT that the Expos did. The stars of the 1994 team included Moises Alou, Larry Walker, Marquis Grissom, Wil Cordero, Ken Hill, and John Wetteland. On August 11, Montreal's record was 74–40. The Expos were the only team in baseball with more than 70 victories. It looked as if Montreal might win its first championship, but an argument between baseball's owners and players stopped the season. They did not settle their differences in time to play the World Series, so the Expos never had the chance to prove how good they really were.

When Greg Harris joined the Expos in 1995, he was nearing the end of his pitching career. He had been in the major leagues since 1981. During that time, he had worn the uniforms of eight different teams. Harris was a good pitcher but never a star. He did not think he would ever be elected to the Hall of Fame.

Before he retired, Harris had a trick up his sleeve. He was ambidextrous—which meant that he could pitch left-handed and right-handed. Though Harris had thrown as a righty for his entire life, he had spent many years practicing as a lefty, too. Harris had one wish. He wanted to pitch from both sides in a big-league game. On September 28, 1995, the Expos agreed to let him try.

Harris came into a game against the Cincinnati Reds wearing a special glove that could be used on either hand. The glove had a thumb at both ends and four finger slots in between them. The first batter Harris faced was righty Reggie Sanders. Harris pitched to him right-handed and got him out. The next batter was lefty Hal Morris. Harris pitched to him left-handed and walked him.

Greg Harris throws a pitch right-handed.

Harris pitched left-handed to the next hitter, Eddie Taubensee, also a lefty. Taubensee grounded out. Harris then switched back to pitching right-handed to retire the final batter of the inning, righty Bret Boone.

The last player to pitch both right-handed and left-handed in a game was Elton Chamberlain, in 1888. In those days, many pitchers did not wear gloves, so it was easier to switch back and forth. Harris accomplished the feat the hard way.

While Harris never made it to the Hall of Fame, the glove he used on that historic day did. It is there today so fans can always remember that special moment.

During their years in Montreal, the Expos had thousands of loyal fans. Unfortunately, Montreal is a "hockey town." Many sports fans there never really got to know baseball. That is one of the reasons why the team moved to Washington, D.C. Baseball has a long history in the country's capital. Fans have been cheering for Washington players for almost 150 years!

In their first year, the Nationals drew nearly three million fans to the ballpark. Three seasons after that, the team rewarded its fans with a beautiful new stadium. The team's mascot, Screech, made the trip to Nationals Park. He is a fan favorite. So are the Racing Presidents. Every game, people dressed up as George Washington, Thomas Jefferson, Abraham Lincoln, and Theodore Roosevelt sprint around the ballpark as the crowd cheers them on.

LEFT: Jefferson, Washington, and Roosevelt race toward the finish line!
ABOVE: Nats fans often get souvenirs such as this Ryan Zimmerman bobblehead at the stadium.

TIMELINE

Bill
Stoneman

MONTREAL   PITCHER

BILL
STONEMAN   EXPOS

1972
Bill Stoneman
pitches his second
no-hitter as an Expo.

1985
Andre Dawson
wins his sixth Gold
Glove in a row.

1969
The team plays its
first season as the
Montreal Expos.

1978
Ross Grimsley
becomes the team's
first 20-game winner.

1990
Delino DeShields gets
four hits in his first
game in the majors.

Delino
DeShields

This pennant celebrates the team's move to Washington, D.C.

2003
Jose Vidro starts in the All-Star Game for the second time.

2010
Stephen Strasburg strikes out 14 hitters in his Nationals *debut*.

1997
Mark Grudzielanek leads the NL with 54 doubles.

2005
The team moves to Washington, D.C. and is renamed the Nationals.

2006
Alfonso Soriano is the first player to hit 40 doubles and 40 homers and steal 40 bases in the same season.

Mark Grudzielanek

Alfonso Soriano holds the 40th base he stole in 2006.

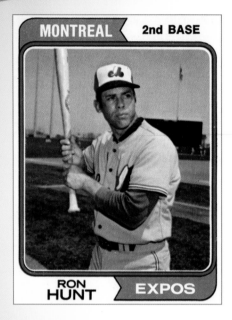

MONTREAL — 2nd BASE

RON HUNT — EXPOS

Ouch!

In 1971, Ron Hunt set a record when he was hit by a pitch 50 times.

Doubly Grand

In 2009, Josh Willingham blasted two home runs with the bases loaded against the Milwaukee Brewers. He became just the 13th player to hit two grand slams in a game.

Giant Killer

Charlie Lea pitched a no-hitter against the San Francisco Giants in May of 1981. In his next game, he shut out the Giants on four hits.

Lucky Seven?

In 2009, the Nationals began the year by losing their first seven games. They ended the season by winning their last seven. No team had ever done that before.

Road Warriors

In 1991, a damaged beam made Montreal's stadium unsafe for fans, so the Expos had to play their home games in the other teams' ballparks. Montreal took the field for 93 games on the road. Normally, a team plays 81 games at home and 81 games away from home.

First and Last

The final batter for the Expos in 2004 was Brad Wilkerson. He was also the first batter for the Nationals in 2005.

Every Second Counts

In 2009, Stephen Strasburg signed his big-league contract 77 seconds before he would have had to return to college for another season. That broke the old record of 93 seconds.

LEFT: Ron Hunt
ABOVE: Brad Wilkerson

"It was fun. I enjoyed it. I would have liked to do it as long as I could."

► **RYAN ZIMMERMAN**, ON HIS 30-GAME HITTING STREAK

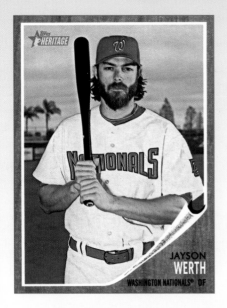

"I love the situation that I'm in. This was where I wanted to be."

► **JAYSON WERTH**, ON WHY HE DECIDED TO JOIN THE NATIONALS

"The dream became a reality today, and I must say this is a very proud day today."

► **GARY CARTER**, ON BEING ELECTED TO THE HALL OF FAME

"Stop working and you're right back to where you came from—nothing."

► **PEDRO MARTINEZ**, ON WHY HE ALWAYS LOOKED FOR NEW WAYS TO GET BATTERS OUT

"What I do is see the ball, hit the ball."
► **VLADIMIR GUERRERO**, ON HIS SIMPLE BATTING STYLE

"I want everybody to feel he has a chance to get into a game when he comes to the ballpark."
► **GENE MAUCH**, ON HOW HE KEPT HIS PLAYERS SHARP

"The key in baseball is getting on base to score runs."
► **TIM RAINES**, ON HIS GOAL AS A HITTER

"If we have more heart and desire than they do, we'll do okay."
► **LARRY WALKER**, ON THE DIFFERENCE BETWEEN WINNING AND LOSING IN THE BIG LEAGUES

LEFT: Jayson Werth
RIGHT: Larry Walker

GREAT DEBATES

People who root for the Expos and the Nationals love to compare their favorite moments, teams, and players. Some debates have been going on for years! How would you settle these classic baseball arguments?

STEPHEN STRASBURG IS THE GREATEST PITCHER IN TEAM HISTORY ...

… because no one can match his fastball or his curve. Strasburg barely looks like he's trying when he pitches. But his fastball regularly travels 100 miles per hour. When he throws his curve, he makes All-Stars look like Little Leaguers. From the first time Strasburg took the mound for the Nats, it was clear he was something special.

DON'T TELL THAT TO PEDRO MARTINEZ ...

… because the numbers don't lie. In 1997, his last year with the Expos, Martinez (**LEFT**) struck out 305 batters and gave up less than two runs a game. He also threw four shutouts. It would also be hard for Strasburg to match Dennis Martinez. He pitched for Montreal from 1986 to 1993 and won 97 games. He led the NL in shutouts in 1991.

... because the 2005 team had talent and heart. Manager Frank Robinson knew how to put a lineup together. Brad Wilkerson was a good **leadoff hitter**, and Jose Guillen and Nick Johnson loved to hit with runners in scoring position. Washington also had a good bullpen. Chad Cordero saved 47 games that year. The 1969 Expos had only 21—as a team!

DON'T BET ON IT. THE 1969 EXPOS WOULD WIN ...

... because they had experienced stars at every position. The team's Opening Day lineup included Rusty Staub, Maury Wills, Mack Jones, Bob Bailey (RIGHT), and Coco Laboy. Ron Fairly and Manny Mota also played for the Expos that year. These players combined to give Montreal great power. The Expos would have clobbered Washington's pitching.

MONTREAL   3rd BASE

BOB BAILEY   EXPOS

The great Expos and Nationals teams and players have left their marks on the record books. These are the "best of the best" …

EXPOS & NATS AWARD WINNERS

WINNER	AWARD	YEAR
Carl Morton	Rookie of the Year*	1970
Gene Mauch	Manager of the Year	1973
Andre Dawson	Rookie of the Year	1977
Dick Williams	Manager of the Year	1979
Gary Carter	All-Star Game MVP	1981
Gary Carter	All-Star Game MVP	1984
Tim Raines	All-Star Game MVP	1987
Buck Rodgers	Manager of the Year	1987
Felipe Alou	Manager of the Year	1994
Pedro Martinez	Cy Young Award	1997
Dmitri Young	Comeback Player of the Year	2007

The annual award given to each league's best first-year player.

Carl Morton

Buck Rodgers

Gary
Carter

EXPOS & NATS ACHIEVEMENTS

ACHIEVEMENT	YEAR
*NL East Second-Half Champions**	*1981*
NL East Champions	*1981*
NL East Champions	*1994*

* The 1981 season was played with first-half and second-half division winners.

Montreal Expos
outfield ELLIS VALENTINE voltigeur
Card Number 7 of 24 - Carte Numéro 7 de 24
© 1981 O-Pee-Chee Co. Ltd. Printed in Canada - Imprimé au Canada

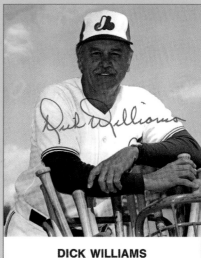

DICK WILLIAMS
Gérant/Manager

TOP: Ellis Valentine was a leader on the 1981 team. **ABOVE**: Dick Williams was the 1979 Manager of the Year. **LEFT**: Moises Alou was a star on the 1994 club.

43

PINPOINTS

The history of a baseball team is made up of many smaller stories. These stories take place all over the map—not just in the city a team calls "home." Match the pushpins on these maps to the **TEAM FACTS**, and you will begin to see the story of the Nationals unfold!

1 Washington, D.C.—*The team has played here since 2005.*

2 Washington, North Carolina—*Ryan Zimmerman was born here.*

3 Atlanta, Georgia—*Mack Jones was born here.*

4 Sanford, Florida—*Tim Raines was born here.*

5 Jefferson City, Missouri—*Steve Rogers was born here.*

6 Helena, Arkansas—*Ellis Valentine was born here.*

7 Oak Park, Illinois—*Bill Stoneman was born here.*

8 San Mateo, California—*John Wetteland was born here.*

9 Los Angeles, California—*The team played in the 1981 NLCS here.*

Vladimir Guerrero

10 Montreal, Quebec, Canada—*The team played here as the Expos from 1969 to 2004.*

11 Granada, Nicaragua—*Dennis Martinez was born here.*

12 Nizao, Dominican Republic—*Vladimir Guerrero was born here.*

GLOSSARY

🔟 **ALL-STAR**—A player who is selected to play in baseball's annual All-Star Game.

🔟 **ALL-STAR GAME**—Baseball's annual game featuring the best players from the American League and National League.

🔟 **AMERICAN LEAGUE**—One of baseball's two major leagues; the AL began play in 1901.

🔟 **BULLPEN**—The area where a team's relief pitchers warm up. This word also describes the group of relief pitchers in this area.

🔟 **CHANGE-UP**—A slow pitch disguised to look like a fastball.

🔟 **CY YOUNG AWARD**—The annual trophy given to each league's best pitcher.

🧠 *DEBUT*—First appearance.

🔟 **DRAFT**—The annual meeting at which teams take turns choosing the best players in high school and college.

🔟 **GOLD GLOVE**—The award given each year to baseball's best fielders.

🔟 **HALL OF FAME**—The museum in Cooperstown, New York, where baseball's greatest players are honored. A player voted into the Hall of Fame is sometimes called a "Hall of Famer."

🧠 *INTERNATIONAL*—Used by people from all over the world.

🧠 *LABOR DISPUTE*—A disagreement between employees and the people they work for.

🔟 **LEADOFF HITTER**—The first hitter in a lineup, or the first hitter in an inning.

🧠 *LOGO*—A symbol or design that represents a company or team.

🔟 **MAJOR LEAGUE BASEBALL (MLB)**—The top level of professional baseball leagues. The American League and National League make up today's major leagues.

🔟 **MINOR LEAGUES**—The many professional leagues that help develop players for the major leagues.

🔟 **MOST VALUABLE PLAYER (MVP)**—The award given each year to each league's top player; an MVP is also selected for the World Series and the All-Star Game.

🔟 **NATIONAL LEAGUE (NL)**—The older of the two major leagues; the NL began play in 1876.

🔟 **NATIONAL LEAGUE CHAMPIONSHIP SERIES (NLCS)**—The playoff series that has decided the NL pennant since 1969.

🔟 **NL EAST**—A group of NL teams that play in the eastern part of the country.

🔟 **NO-HITTER**—A game in which a team does not get a hit.

🔟 **PENNANT**—A league championship. The term comes from the triangular flag awarded to each season's champion, beginning in the 1870s.

🔟 **PLAYER-MANAGER**—A player who also manages his team.

🧠 *PROSPECTS*—Young athletes who are expected to become stars.

🔟 **ROOKIE**—A player in his first season.

🔟 **SAVED**—Recorded the last out or outs in a team's win. A relief pitcher on the mound at the end of a close victory is credited with a "save."

🔟 **SHUTOUTS**—Games in which one team does not score a run.

🧠 *STRIKE*—A work stoppage by employees. Workers go on strike to get better treatment from their employer.

🧠 *SUMMER OLYMPICS*—An international sports competition held every four years.

🔟 **WORLD SERIES**—The world championship series played between the American League and National League pennant winners.

EXTRA INNINGS

TEAM SPIRIT introduces a great way to stay up to date with your team! Visit our **EXTRA INNINGS** link and get connected to the latest and greatest updates. **EXTRA INNINGS** serves as a young reader's ticket to an exclusive web page—with more stories, fun facts, team records, and photos of the Nationals. Content is updated during and after each season. The **EXTRA INNINGS** feature also enables readers to send comments and letters to the author! Log onto:

www.norwoodhousepress.com/library.aspx

and click on the tab: **TEAM SPIRIT** to access **EXTRA INNINGS**.

Read all the books in the series to learn more about professional sports. For a complete listing of the baseball, basketball, football, and hockey teams in the **TEAM SPIRIT** series, visit our website at:

www.norwoodhousepress.com/library.aspx

ON THE ROAD

WASHINGTON NATIONALS
1500 South Capitol Street Southeast
Washington, D.C. 20003
(202) 675-6287
washington.nationals.mlb.com

**NATIONAL BASEBALL
HALL OF FAME AND MUSEUM**
25 Main Street
Cooperstown, New York 13326
(888) 425-5633
www.baseballhalloffame.org

ON THE BOOKSHELF

To learn more about the sport of baseball, look for these books at your library or bookstore:

- Augustyn, Adam (editor). *The Britannica Guide to Baseball.* New York, NY: Rosen Publishing, 2011.

- Dreier, David. *Baseball: How It Works.* North Mankato, MN: Capstone Press, 2010.

- Stewart, Mark. *Ultimate 10: Baseball.* New York, NY: Gareth Stevens Publishing, 2009.

ABOUT THE AUTHOR

MARK STEWART has written more than 50 books on baseball and over 150 sports books for kids. He grew up in New York City during the 1960s rooting for the Yankees and Mets, and was lucky enough to meet players from both teams. Mark comes from a family of writers. His grandfather was Sunday Editor of *The New York Times,* and his mother was Articles Editor of *Ladies' Home Journal* and *McCall's.* Mark has profiled hundreds of athletes over the past 25 years. He has also written several books about his native New York and New Jersey, his home today. Mark is a graduate of Duke University, with a degree in history. He lives and works in a home overlooking Sandy Hook, New Jersey. You can contact Mark through the Norwood House Press website.